Once Upon A New Moon

Katharina Notarianni

Copyright

© 2017 Katharina Notarianni. All rights reserved.

This book or any portion thereof may not be reproduced, used or stored in any manner whatsoever without the express written permission of the publisher except for the use of brief quotations in a book review.

Library of Congress Catalog Number: 2017910744

ISBN-13: 978-0982105290 / ISBN-10: 0982105290 (paperback)

1. Poetry 2. Shamanism 3. Spirituality
4. Philosophy 5. Creativity

For academic discounts email info@healingtimebooks.com
Kindle eBook available through Amazon.com

Images and Shamanic Creative Works
by Katharina Notarianni unless noted otherwise

Cover image of 'Full Moon'
by Katharina and John Notarianni

Published by

Healing Time Books

www.healingtimebooks.com

Printed in the U.S.A.

Dedication

These poems are dedicated to my husband
John Notarianni
who came upon me in the midst of writing them

and married me under a redwood tree.

He is my partner and inspires me

to be more of who I truly am.

He continues to show me even now

the importance of loving oneself

and what being loving is all about.

'Deer Medicine' Leather Pouch
by Katharina Notarianni (1993)

Acknowledgments

I have been inspired by my friends who have honored me by publishing their own creative works through my publishing company, Healing Time Books. These are the authors I so admire, who enrich my life immeasurably, and to whom I give my heartfelt thanks for their friendship and continued confidence in me:

Drs. E. Reenah McGill and Marianne Zaugg published their groundbreaking health book 'Eat Right, Lose Weight - Introducing the 5 Element Nutrition and Hypnosis System' with me, followed by Reenah publishing her own collection of poems, 'Poetry MS – Volumes 1 & 2.'

Richard C. Richards, a fellow iris lover and philosopher, published his entertaining yet serious book 'A Philosopher Looks At The Sense of Humor', followed by his collection of poetry, 'Poems That Almost Got Away - Reflections on Death and Life.'

Suellen M. Fast, poetria, musician and creator of innovative learning tools, chanced upon me at an iris sale at Balboa Park in San Diego and instantly hired me to publish her beautiful collection of poems 'Poetry For A

Acknowledgments

Young Girl' and her book of affirmations 'I am A Young Girl.'

Marilyn Marlow, artist, photographer, and creative whirlwind published her bilingual illustrated children's story 'Love and Light ~ A Creation Myth' in English with Spanish translation, also available in Spanish with English translation with the title 'Amor y Luz ~ Un Mito de la Creación.'

There are numerous others to acknowledge, in particular my dear family and friends, for supporting all of my phases of creativity over the years. Thank you for all your love. John, especially, helps keep me on the straight and narrow. He pays impeccable attention to detail, which makes all the difference.

I also specifically want to acknowledge my brother Benjamin (Ben) Huber of Graphics Worldwide who was instrumental in getting me started when he printed my full color 'Beauty of Irises' book in gorgeous rich colors on quality paper before print-on-demand services were readily available.

Acknowledgments

Working with gentle, kind and brilliant people has given me courage, and so I finally took the time to refine my poems written so long ago. Interestingly the theme of these poems is still currently at play in my life. What a surprise!

'The Universe' Obsidian Sphere
by Katharina Notarianni (1994)

Contents

Copyright ii
Dedication. iii
Acknowledgments v
Contents ix
Introduction xi
Once Upon A New Moon
   Desert Dreaming 1
   I Seek My Self 3
   A New Way To Love 9
   White Buffalo Calf Woman Calling Me Home . 13
   Lemurian Dreams 15
   Opening To Change 19
   Coming Alive 21
   Return To The Goddess 25
About The Author 27
Books by Katharina Notarianni 31

'Vision Quest' Medicine Wheel
by Katharina Notarianni (1994)

Introduction

These poems were written during a time in my life when I was seeking to understand life, the universe and who I am. That time is ongoing. I am still in process, perhaps forever so.

I endeavored to become more of my Self through shamanic journeying and these poems were the outcome of a New Moon creative group. At the time, I was working full-time at a biotech start-up and was relieved to have a mechanism that helped me detach from the fast pace there to explore my own creativity. I was delighted to find at the end of the process I had produced something I was proud of, namely, this book.

During my shamanic training, I was inspired to craft "medicine" items for myself and others. I gathered feathers, bones, stones and shells as I walked on the beach, in the redwoods and mountains of San Francisco and then created something magical in the process of connecting with the spirit of the animal. Throughout this book you will find examples of items I made in trance - medicine wheels commemorating a vision quest, a rattle made

Introduction

from a sea gourd and sea lion fur, a medicine pouch made from deer hide, and a prayer flag are all meaningful to me because of the shamanic creative process which brought insights and inspiration. Later I was gifted items made specifically for me - a kangaroo skin drum made by Australian shaman Firesun-Phyllis Thorpe, and a white leather beaded medicine bag beautifully hand crafted by Robin-Panther Woman.

It was during the years of my shamanic training that I met my true love, John Notarianni, who wandered to America from Australia and found me. It was remarkable that this creative process, which involved reflecting on who I have been, who am I really, and who I am becoming, opened the door to receiving more and more of the love we share. Shortly after we met I began channeling Tara and continue to do so for myself and others. John has been key to my development as a channel. He is the ultimate question asker with his avid interest in metaphysics and curiosity about how the world works, and I am most grateful to him for his love and support.

Introduction

Rereading the poems after so many years was enlightening, and I am reminded how valuable the shamanic creative process was in helping me connect to the "more" than me and therefore to better understand my Self from a more loving perspective, that of my higher self and soul. The wonderful thing about poetry, is that there isn't a "right way" to write poems. I felt free to simply express what was in my heart and mind without judgment.

I hope my poems inspire you to vision quest, to discover more of who you truly are and begin your own creative journey of self expression.

Once Upon A New Moon

'Owl Medicine' Rattle
Mexican Indian Artist (1995)

Desert Dreaming

Great horned Owl, Spirit of the North
Carry me South to the desert
Of my Soul.

The stars glimmer in the night sky
Above me
As I perch on sandstone

Owl has a message for me
I cannot hear
I see myself forlorn
Weeping in despair

The Ancestors call me to the fire
    To share in the warm glow
I gaze into their wise faces
    Familiar and strong
I invite the fire into my belly
    To spark the passion
    That lies dormant

Desert Dreaming

Spirit drummers drum

Spirit dancers sway

I move to the sound, wildly at first

Then slowly with the others

I belong

This I now know

And so it is time

To journey back

I take flight

Owl magic carries me home

In silence and knowing that

The journey is just beginning

I Seek My Self

Black beak

Black eyes

Scanning the prairie for prey

Seeking clues to nourish the Soul

White masked one among the crowd

Catches my eye

Appears then disappears

What is your mask? I ask

The face transforms into Vulture

Bald with a sharp stare

Piercing deep into me

What do you see? I ask

I must be still and look within

Where my answer waits for me

The scene changes

To a skier racing

I Seek My Self

Swiftly downwards then up again
Flying through the air
A crash landing, then laughter
As I realize I am not hurt
I unbuckle the skies from my feet

What shackles me? I ask
I replay the scene in my mind's eye
And understand
My fear is not of flying high
But of crashing
The crash of failure and humiliation
That is sure to follow

I have flown
I have fallen
I have survived
    Yet the fear exists
    It controls me
    It shackles my will

I Seek My Self

To fly
To soar free

The scene changes once more
I see the desert sky
Violet hues
Bathe the mountains and the stones

I am She-Bear who dreams of
A beautiful river flowing
Through lush greenery
I thirst for more
The stones speak
And lead me to an oasis

I am alone
I am at peace
I dream of Star beings
And in soft cozy darkness
I remember

I Seek My Self

I am the Warrior
      Unrelenting
      Unyielding
Who seeks her Self
      With valor
      And courage
Fighting to free her will

It is my Self who awaits me
In the silence
I am not alone
I am my Self
I am free

'Essence'
by Katharina Notarianni (1993)

'Sea Otters' Joy' Medicine Rattle
by Katharina Notarianni (1995)

A New Way To Love

The day began with a choice
    To feel and heal the pain
    Through caretaking
    Or nurturing

At the time, it was not an easy choice
Trying to carry another's burden in the name of love
Often seen as admirable, loving
Yet I could see this was no solution

It seemed my friend's pain was splitting him apart
He held it tightly in his heart
Unable to break down, to be free

I wanted to help him
Though this meant he would lose control
    Of himself, his pain

A walk on the beach to ease the strain
    We separated

A New Way To Love

Each choosing to go within
For healing

Soaking in the sun's rays deep into my heart
Clearing out my troubled feelings
Needing to regain my lost sense of peace
Recognizing that to take on pain not mine
Emotions not my own
Weighed me down
Made me resentful

I journeyed to a place within
To release this heart worn burden
And emerged back on the beach
No longer in a cloud
I felt clear and calm
Centered
Carefree

A New Way To Love

My friend approached me, smiling

He felt better

Thanking me

For the space

I gave

'Starbuck' Medicine Bag
by Panther Woman (1995)

White Buffalo Calf Woman Calling Me Home

With wolf at my side

I ride the winds of Spirit

To a place within

That once was my homeland

I see the mountains high

Rich with trees and flowing streams

The cool North wind whispers to me

"White Buffalo Calf Woman is coming"

I respond to the call

And take my place in the circle

I am ready

To welcome Her

She comes to me

With eyes glimmering like stars

She smiles her gentle smile

Inviting me

White Buffalo Calf Woman Calling Me Home

I feel the spirit of the Ancestors
As they fill my heart with love
And bring a peaceful calm
I am released from past refrains

With newfound gladness
I welcome those I love to join me
How could I have every doubted
They would come

I gaze around the circle at their familiar faces
Smiling at me
My heart opens wide to them
As a continuous stream of joy enfolds us

White Buffalo Calf Woman reminds me
To pause and experience
This circle of love
This feeling of coming home

Lemurian Dreams

I am the Wise Woman
Receiving the light of the Goddess
And flowing it into my creation

I am the Newborn Babe
Innately seeking nourishment to grow strong
With love and trust

I am the Timber Wolf
Calmly standing still among the trees
Stealthily observing the valley below
Gauging whether to engage or flee

I am the Nordic Warrior
Battle axe in hand, mace in the other
Spinning round and round and round
Banishing fear and darkness
That keeps me locked in a survival stance

Lemurian Dreams

I am the Seeker
Sprawled on a rugged mountainside
Battling with the choice to grow from my discomfort
I welcome this gentle peaceful transformation

I am the Priestess
Standing on broad stone steps of the sacred temple I tend
Content in knowing my destiny
Easily rising above petty nuisances
nipping at my hem like little mice

As I reflect on who I am
And look forward to who I am becoming
The Goddess calls me to remember always
I am the Lemurian Dreamer
I dream the dreams

'Ancient One ~ Grandfather'
Lemurian Dreamer's Companion Crystal

'Shadow Work' Prayer Flag
by Katharina Notarianni (1994)

Opening To Change

Butterflies, bright orange and black monarchs
Flutter around and cling to the stone vessel of water
Like ideas hovering around a deep well of emotions
Seeking transformation

As I open to being loved, love pours into my life
Then without warning, fear grips my heart
      with its steely tentacles
Fearing I am not enough
It whispers
I do not deserve

How can I explain this love that suddenly appeared?
It requires that I commit to loving my Self first
To conquer these odd fears
And change the beliefs holding me prisoner

As I open to change the way I have always been
I realize the truth

Opening To Change

Cocooned in a protective layer of numbness
I avoid pain and humiliation

As I release my need to control the outcome
I am free to heal, and only then
Can I shine my light into another's heart
To love and be loved

I am changed forever

Coming Alive

I step into the fire

Flames of passion and life licking the soles of my feet

Igniting a spark which quickly grows to warm my Soul

The flames burn away a crusty layer of conditioned behavior

Then begin to erode the masks I wear

Disguising the fear that within me is nothing more than

Emptiness and nothingness

As I expand my Self beyond my physical form

Becoming fluid as water

And wide as the sky

Yet grounded in the Earth

I look into the space within me

Mentally turning my Self inside out

I discover a new world yet to be explored

Waiting to guide me into the Void

Stands the Gatekeeper, a warrior

Staff in hand

Coming Alive

Wind whips his hair

With a sparkle in his eye

He patiently awaits my commitment to follow

Promising adventure

A return to my true Self

I make the choice

Guided by imagination

I answer this longing deep in my heart

To come alive

'Metamorphosis' Medicine Wheel
by Katharina Notarianni (1995)

'Golden Feather'
by Katharina Notarianni (1995)

Return To The Goddess

On Eagle's wings of golden light

I return to the beginning of this life

A child held in the arms of the Goddess

Receiving nourishment from Her love

I am and was always whole and complete

'Shaman Drum' for Katharina
by Firesun Phyliss Thorpe (1998)

About The Author

Katharina Notarianni

Author, Publisher, Editor, Photographer & Spiritual Channel

Once Upon A New Moon, a collection of poems by Katharina Notarianni, were written utilizing a shamanic creative process, whereby she journeyed to other realms and brought back imagery and profound insights which she translated into poetry while still in trance.

Katharina Notarianni's background as a channel began with her interest in metaphysics. She incorporated shamanic studies, Reiki energy, working with crystals and making gem essences, Yuen Method, and channeling on her spiritual path. She is best known for channeling Tara, who brings peace and love to all who call upon her.

Katharina Notarianni began her publishing career with her first book, 'The Beauty of Irises,' a gardening picture book focused on tall bearded irises which she grew in her own garden and was inspired to photograph and

About The Author

write about. Setting out to publish this book inspired her to start Healing Time Books, a publishing company to help authors like herself make the most of today's digital technologies to publish their works. She loves working with creative people on topics dear to their heart. To find out more about how Healing Time Books Publishing Services can help you move forward on your project, visit www.healingtimebooks.com.

Katharina currently volunteers as president of the San Diego Iris Society. Previously, she served as vice president and editor, and continues to serve as webmaster. Katharina also served as editor for Region 15 of the American Iris Society for several years.

Katharina and John live in the mountains of San Diego where they enjoy its ideal climate and wildlife right outside their front door. California quail and tree frogs, coyote and roadrunner, cottontail rabbit, hummingbird and red tail hawk are frequent visitors.

About The Author

'Eagles Dance'
by Katharina & John Notarianni (2009)

'White Tara'
by Katharina Notarianni (2008)

Books
by Katharina Notarianni

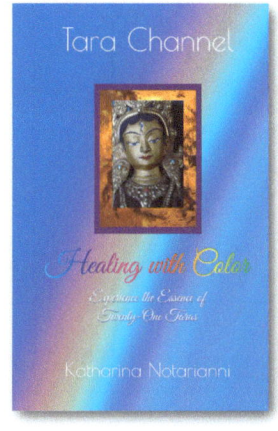

'Healing with Color'

Experience the Essence of Twenty-One Taras

by Katharina Notarianni

(ISBN 978-0982105276)

'Healing with Color', by Tara as channeled through Katharina Notarianni, is a collection of meditative journeys that focus on healing through the use of visualizing colors on your journey of becoming more of who you truly are.

Recommended as a 21-day process, simply read and experience one specific color each day and follow the guidance that is given. Let the key words and affirmations guide and support you thereafter, when you wish to focus upon a particular energy to activate something specific within yourself and your life.

Tara is a universal expression of the goddess energy not tied to any particular culture or religion. She comes with love and peace, to share her wisdom with us as we continue our journey to become more of who we truly are.

Books
by Katharina Notarianni

Through Katharina Notarianni, known as the Tara Channel, Tara brings peace and love to all, and her interactions bring a breadth and depth of insight to those who seek her counsel.

For more information about Tara, please visit www.tarachannel.com.

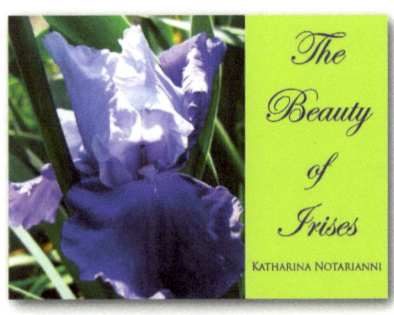

'The Beauty of Irises'

by Katharina Notarianni

(ISBN 978-0982105207)

The Beauty of Irises by Katharina Notarianni is a gardening picture book that delights the eyes. Let The Beauty of Irises inspire you and lift your spirit. Each photograph brings the beauty of the garden into your living room. This book makes a great gift. With over 100 full color photographs of stunning irises, 'The Beauty of Irises' also includes advice on growing and landscaping with irises. Many irises, particularly the bearded varieties,

Books
by Katharina Notarianni

are perfect for the drought tolerant garden. This book lists reputable commercial sources for procuring quality irises for your garden.

Katharina Notarianni's books are currently available on Amazon.com. For academic discounts, please contact info@healingtimebooks.com.

www.ingramcontent.com/pod-product-compliance
Lightning Source LLC
Chambersburg PA
CBHW041823220426
43666CB00004BA/61